T0011866

Life Cycle of a Butterfly

by Meg Gaertner

FOCUS READERS®

PIONEER

www.focusreaders.com

Copyright © 2022 by Focus Readers®, Lake Elmo, MN 55042. All rights reserved. No part of this book may be reproduced or utilized in any form or by any means without written permission from the publisher.

Focus Readers is distributed by North Star Editions:
sales@northstareditions.com | 888-417-0195

Produced for Focus Readers by Red Line Editorial.

Photographs ©: iStockphoto, cover, 1, 4, 7, 8, 11, 12, 15, 17, 18; Shutterstock Images, 21

Library of Congress Cataloging-in-Publication Data
Names: Gaertner, Meg, author.
Title: Life cycle of a butterfly / by Meg Gaertner.
Description: Lake Elmo, MN : Focus Readers, [2022] | Series: Life
   cycles | Includes index. | Audience: Grades 2-3
Identifiers: LCCN 2021003716 (print) | LCCN 2021003717 (ebook) | ISBN
   9781644938263 (hardcover) | ISBN 9781644938720 (paperback) | ISBN
   9781644939185 (ebook) | ISBN 9781644939628 (pdf)
Subjects: LCSH: Butterflies--Life cycles--Juvenile literature.
Classification: LCC QL544.2 .G338 2022 (print) | LCC QL544.2 (ebook) |
   DDC 595.78/9156--dc23
LC record available at https://lccn.loc.gov/2021003716
LC ebook record available at https://lccn.loc.gov/2021003717

Printed in the United States of America
Mankato, MN
082021

About the Author

Meg Gaertner enjoys reading, writing, dancing, and being outside. She lives in Minnesota.

Table of Contents

Chapter 1

Egg

A butterfly completely changes forms during its life. The young form looks very different from the adult form. This change is called **metamorphosis**.

Butterflies start as eggs. A **female** butterfly lays many eggs at once. This happens in the spring, summer, or fall. She lays the eggs on plants. The eggs are tiny.

Fun Fact

Some butterfly eggs are as small as the period at the end of this sentence.

egg

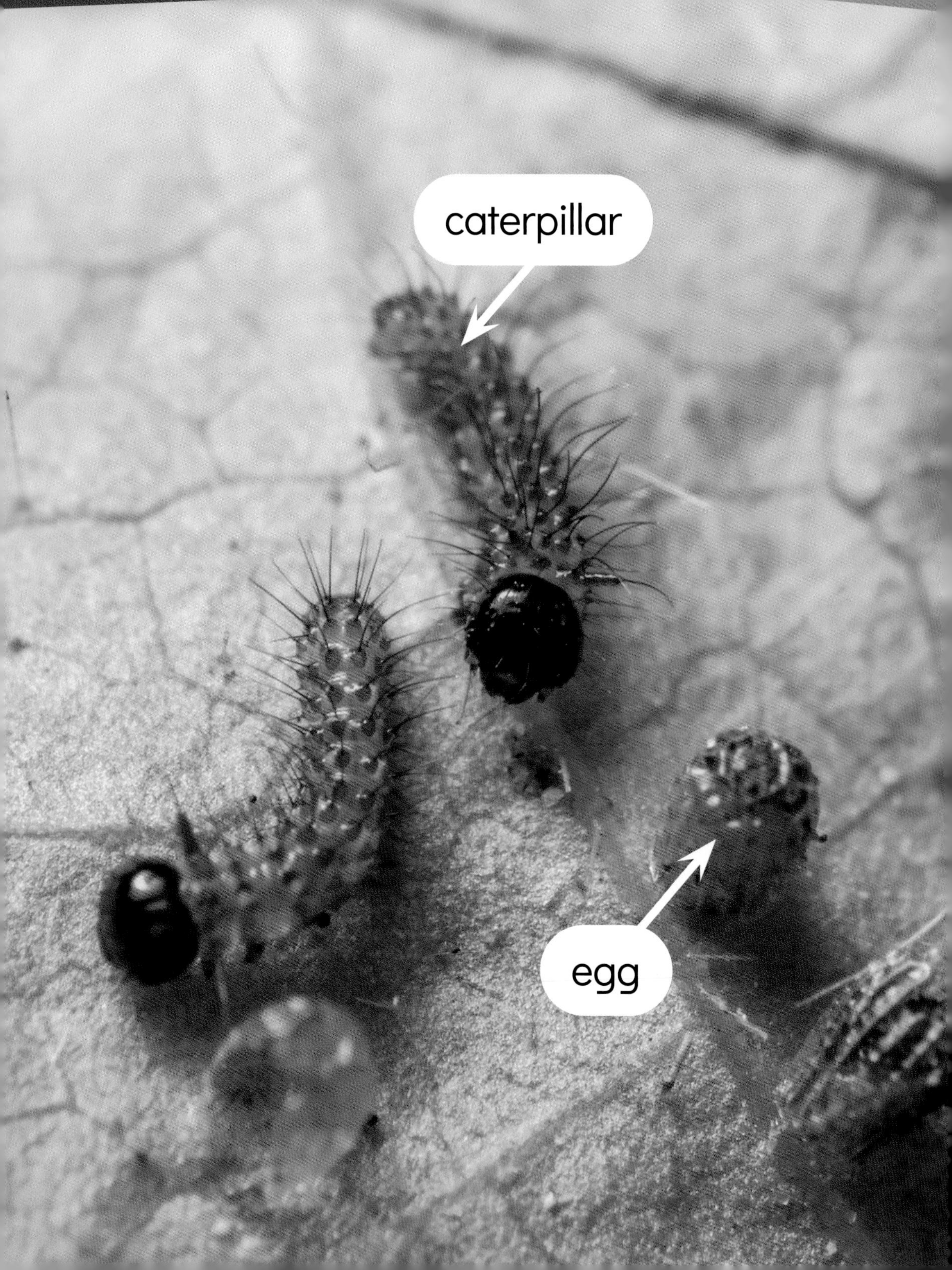
caterpillar
egg

Chapter 2

Caterpillar

The eggs **hatch**. Caterpillars come out. A caterpillar is a butterfly **larva**. It has a long, thin body. It has many short legs. And it has strong jaws.

The caterpillar eats a lot. It eats the plant around it. Then it eats nearby plants. It stores all that food in its body.

The caterpillar grows. As it gets bigger, its skin splits. The caterpillar **sheds** its skin four or five times.

chrysalis

Chapter 3

Chrysalis

The caterpillar stops eating. It enters the **pupa** stage. A chrysalis forms around it. This covering is hard. It protects the caterpillar.

The chrysalis hangs from a twig. Or it is hidden by leaves. From the outside, nothing seems to be happening. But big changes are taking place.

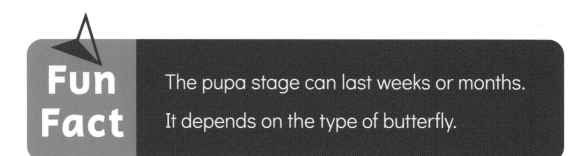

Fun Fact

The pupa stage can last weeks or months. It depends on the type of butterfly.

Big Changes

Inside the chrysalis, the caterpillar breaks down. It **digests** itself. New parts form. These parts include legs, wings, and eyes. When it is ready, an adult butterfly comes out of the chrysalis. It splits the chrysalis skin. Or it chews its way out.

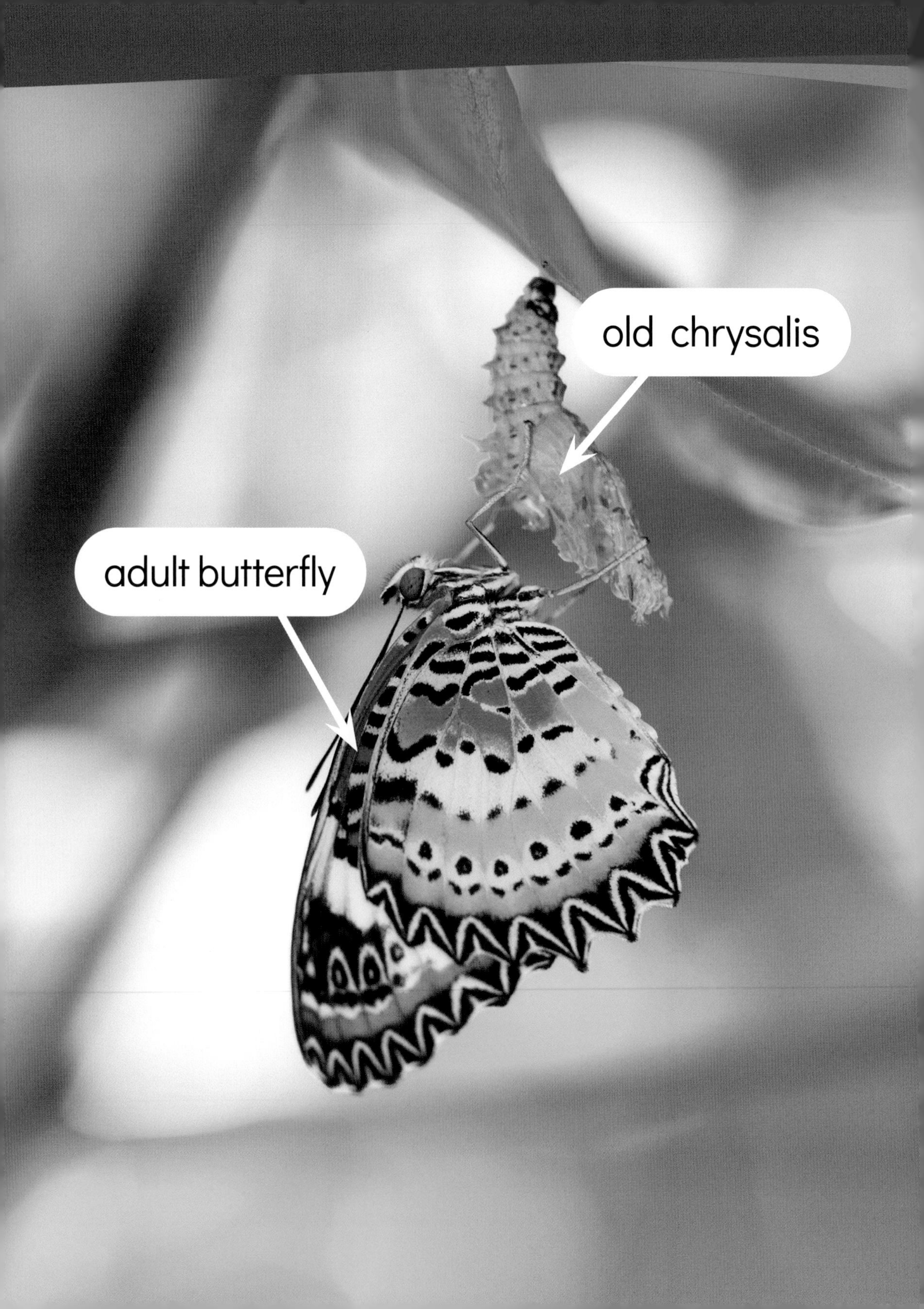
old chrysalis
adult butterfly

Chapter 4

Adult

Adult butterflies have long legs and **antennae**. They also have large, colorful wings. Some butterflies live for one week. Others live several months.

Adult butterflies fly around. Some drink the nectar from flowers. This sweet drink gives them energy to fly.

Female butterflies look for certain plants. They lay many eggs on the plants. The life cycle begins again.

Fun Fact

Adult butterflies cannot grow.

Life Cycle Stages

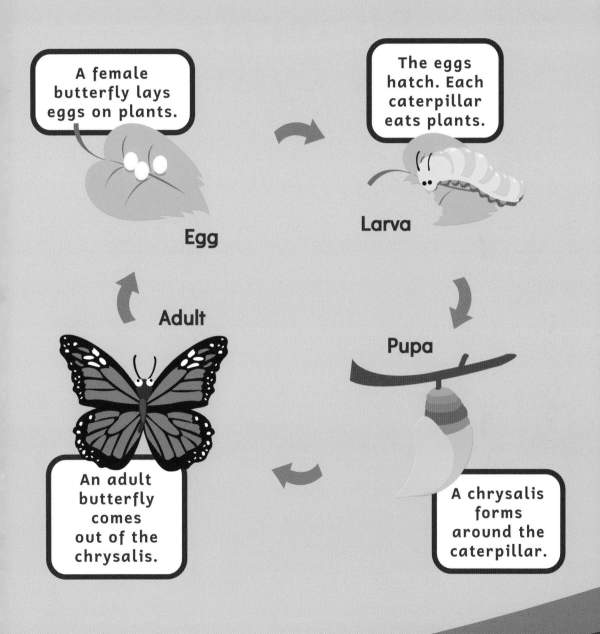

A female butterfly lays eggs on plants.

Egg

The eggs hatch. Each caterpillar eats plants.

Larva

Adult

Pupa

An adult butterfly comes out of the chrysalis.

A chrysalis forms around the caterpillar.

FOCUS ON
Butterfly Life Cycles

Write your answers on a separate piece of paper.

1. Write a sentence describing what happens inside a chrysalis.

2. Which stage of the life cycle do you find most interesting? Why?

3. In which stage do caterpillars get a hard, protective covering?
   A. egg
   B. larva
   C. pupa

4. Why do caterpillars eat so much?
   A. They use the food for energy to lay eggs.
   B. They need energy to grow new parts during the pupa stage.
   C. They use the food for energy to fly around.

Answer key on page 24.

Glossary

antennae
Long, thin body parts on an insect's head. The parts are used for sensing.

digests
Breaks down food into bits that the body can use.

female
Able to have babies or lay eggs.

hatch
To break open so a young animal can come out.

larva
The young, active form of an insect.

metamorphosis
A change from a young form to a completely different adult form.

pupa
The inactive form of an insect. During this stage, the insect changes from a larva to an adult.

sheds
Allows skin to fall off.

To Learn More

BOOKS

Dunn, Mary R. *A Butterfly's Life Cycle*. North Mankato, MN: Capstone Press, 2018.

London, Martha. *Butterflies*. Lake Elmo, MN: Focus Readers, 2021.

NOTE TO EDUCATORS

Visit **www.focusreaders.com** to find lesson plans, activities, links, and other resources related to this title.

Index

Answer Key: **1.** Answers will vary; **2.** Answers will vary; **3.** C; **4.** B